Fast Track

Strategic Planning

By John Dame

Tim Levy and Associates

2015

Title: *Fast Track Strategic Planning*

Author: *John Dame*

Published by: *Tim Levy and Associates*

First Edition, August 2014

Published in the United States of America

Contents

SECTION TWO

WHAT IS STRATEGIC PLANNING?

SECTION THREE

PRACTICAL MATTERS

SECTION FOUR

WHAT CAN GO WRONG?

SECTION FIVE

SUCCESS STORIES

SKIP THE SWOT ANALYSIS, AND
JUST CUT THE ROPE ALREADY!

Section One

The Introduction

This book is about an accelerated strategic planning technique I have developed over the course of three decades as a CEO, coach and mentor. I've called it Fast Track Strategic Planning because it happens so much more quickly than traditional processes. It yields similar and sometimes even better results without wasting time on long meetings and repeatedly covering the same ground.

I have written this book with one specific intention. That is to lay out this process for you in simple, easy and precise language so that you can do this process for yourself. I'm hoping you'll reap the benefits of rapid planning in your own business endeavors. Whether you are a small business or a multi-million dollar enterprise, I believe you will benefit enormously from my Fast Track Strategic Planning technique. I have seen the proof over and over.

At the same time, I have a particular soap box, a particular passion which I want to share with you. That is a passion for purpose. I like to think that my work will leave the planet in some way a better place. I am hoping that idea will resonate with youon some level, and that you'll use this process to accelerate down the pathway to fulfilling your own purpose.

Often times we find ourselves feeling powerless against the enormous problems facing our country – and indeed, our world. We wonder what we can do, as individuals or as groups. I believe we can indeed do something to help. Each small step can be a step in the right direction, and with swift and effective planning, these steps can follow sooner rather than later.

More and more these days, I find myself working as a bridge between two groups of people. On the one hand, I spend a lot of time with the current CEOs of large companies. These are generally, although not always, people of my own generation. On the other hand, we have the so-called Millennial generation – the emerging leaders. These young people, who are currently between twenty and thirty years old, are beginning to populate not only the workplace but the leadership teams as well. They are young, fast-thinking, entrepreneurial and idealistic. In many ways, they are the opposite of the generation that reached adulthood in the materialistic 1980s.

This change has been coming for a while. It was possible to hire someone maybe 50 or 100 years ago and have them work pretty much as a cog in your machine. They would work tirelessly as a link in your chain without much questioning. You you do your work to make a living, get your pay check, and that's that. You follow orders and work hard.

The Millennials are changing this. They are saying, "No matter how much you pay me, it's not enough if there is a lack of purpose."

There's a huge gap of understanding between these two groups, and it's a particular passion of mine to play some part in bringing them together. I enjoy combining the strengths of each group. One group brings experience and wisdom. The other brings idealism, fresh new insight and passion for change.

Together, these two groups will change the world.

OVERVIEW

This book is divided into five sections.

1. In **Section One**, we look into just who I am, where I came from and what I bring to this particular process.

2. In **Section Two**, we jump into Strategic Planning; what it is and why it is a priority for you and your business.

3. In **Section Three**, we move into the specific steps and details of the Fast Track Strategic Planning process itself. We take them one by one, showing how one step builds on another to make a cohesive whole.

4. In **Section Four**, we look into the traps and potential pitfalls of the process and how to avoid them.

5. Finally, in **Section Five**, we look at some success stories and wrap up the book, giving you some additional resources and salient next steps.

I trust you will enjoy reading this book and putting the process into practice as much as I have enjoyed writing it.

Let's begin our journey together by answering the question a colleague and friend once asked me quite seriously: "John, why should I bother to do a strategic plan in the first place?"

THE IMPORTANCE OF PLANNING

Without a plan, it's impossible to determine where you will end up.

There are many businesses that have no particular plan, but that still end up in an okay place. If you want a greater level of confidence in your ability to have some control over *how* you want to get somewhere, then you are going to need to plan.

You need to spend the time to think about that desired destination, and to consider how you are going to get there quickly, easily and in an organized manner. There could be a lot of different options for reaching your goal, and you want to use the one that's most efficient.

A TRAVEL STORY

Let me illustrate my point through a quick story.

I have some good friends who are cheap. They like to save money in just about any way they can, even at the cost of some inconvenience to themselves. When they travel, they usually schedule a flight that's cheaper. You know the one - it's that plane route that has two or more layovers.

They want to go from Pennsylvania to Florida, but they'll go first to Detroit, then they'll go to Atlanta, and then finally they'll go to Florida, and the whole trip will take twelve hours. They still get to their destination, but it took twelve hours to get there!

If I choose to make the same trip, I get on a direct flight straight from Pennsylvania to Florida and it takes me three hours. I like the three hour flights a lot better than I like the twelve hour flights. They save me time and inconvenience, and that's the real difference in business planning. You can take an organization in a specific direction, as easily and efficiently as you can, or you can just allow the force of nature to blow you about in the air, and allow things to happen as and when they will.

- If you want specific results, in the shortest time and in the most efficient manner, then plan.

- If you're comfortable with random results, and have no fixed timeline or route in mind, then don't plan.

PURPOSE IN PLANNING

In today's world, very few people want to go to work just to make a buck for the company that employs them. Certainly, everybody needs to be financially secure and earning a living that will allow them to meet the minimum standards of comfort. Beyond that, I believe that most individuals who work like to have a defining purpose beyond their pay check.

There's a definite reason why people want to work every day and feel they're achieving something or making a difference. Getting to know the purpose of the organization in human terms – that is, creating a narrative – allows them to connect at a more emotional level with the organization. It's going beyond the superficial idea of "I work here because I want to make money."

When you disconnect from purpose, you end up being disappointed. Companies that do so say things like **"We've had ten or fifteen years of disappointment at the leadership level because it was felt that the ends justified the means.** Making money was everything, and so financial reward was the ultimate end of everything. No one seemed to care about anything else."

These organizations allow themselves to believe that making a dollar is their purpose. They become cold and impersonal. The *goodness* that can come from purpose – and that can guide you to making a difference to the world – is missing.

I don't ever want to disconnect from purpose. I understand that companies have to make money and there's nothing wrong with making money. It's a necessary activity in the 21st Century. But I do think making money is an outcome of having a great purpose, a great vision, and a great strategy. I think it's an outcome, and a valuable outcome, but not the only one. **You see, money and purpose are not mutually exclusive.** It's not as if you can have only one of them.

The companies that generally have the greatest purpose, and the greatest ability to connect most of the employees to that purpose, are the ones that have a greater chance of succeeding and keeping that great talent working for them. More and more, great talent is aligned with passion, fire and purpose.

It is no longer sufficient to define some arbitrary financial goal as the primary and singular outcome for the organization.

In the workplace environment today, study after study has been done to discover the level of interest and engagement in employees across the country. The results of the studies tell a grim story. Only one-third of the people who work in any organization in the United States are actively engaged, which means they're emotionally attached to their product or service. This means that two-thirds of all employees are not ready and willing to give their best effort and their best talent to the job at hand. Do some of these people work for or with you? Are you one of them?

This lack of engagement is creating frustration for leadership, because the leaders are wondering why their people just show up for work, punch in, punch out, and fail to have a commitment to the company. According to the studies, a disengaged person does about half the work that an engaged person does over the course of a day. The work is nothing but a means to an end. How do things change when purpose is brought into the picture?

When an organization defines itself in terms other than a financial metric, that does not mean the paycheck is unimportant. In other words, there still needs to be a financial component encouraging the arrival at the destination. Purpose says if we're doing the right things, we should be financially secure. Why? Because if we are financially doing the right things, if we're making good decisions, then we're able to make a significant social impact.

- We can be invested in the local and wider community

- We can be invested in our people

- We can help develop our people

- We can give back so much, in some manner or another

Companies that do not have financial health are generally not giving back to their people or to the community. So financial health needs to be one of the components, and an important one. But if it's the only important metric measured, then people disconnect.

Everybody looks at your goals, whether you like it or not.

Part of my background is in the world of radio. In the radio station industry they tune to the channel, "What's in it for me?" or WIIFM. They look at every goal that you have with that idea clearly in mind. If a listener doesn't like a particular radio channel, they tune it out and never tune back in.

There are lots of reasons why a company needs to have good financial health. It makes things better for everyone at every level of the company, and also helps consumers. But along with that, the destination or vision needs to have other elements that are appealing to people from the standpoint of purpose.

THE HYDROWORX STORY

Let me tell you another little story to illustrate the point.

Hydroworx is a company that makes therapeutic pools. This is an important product, since the pools have a wide range of medical applications as well as athletic and fitness applications. In other words, these pools can change and improve lives!

This company wanted to continue to do well, and so developed a metric that aligned with their vision of the company beyond the almighty dollar. That metric was this: **they decided to change the lives of fifty thousand patients a day**.

Think of that! Having an effect on the lives of fifty thousand patients and their families is an incredible amount of impact. If the company could have a positive impact on this many patients a day, they knew they'd sell the heck out of Hydroworx pools. If that many people were using their pools every day, the company would make a dramatic impact on the health and wellness of a large number of people, both physically and spiritually. They can make a positive difference and help people achieve their goals of rehabilitation and fitness, bringing them closer to a normal life and eventual transition to more independent living. So that's the image they use as their purpose, and it drives everything that they do. Make money? Sure. Help people? That's the story that drives everything now.

Before they took up this vision, they had a financial vision that said that they wanted to do X number of million dollars, topline revenue and profits.

This did not resonate as well with the people in the organization because with Hydroworx, the purpose is very visual. Numbers on a balance sheet are just numbers. Now, let's say you see someone who can hardly walk, through injury, or even obesity, which is a huge issue in the United States and the rest of the developed world today. Then this person steps into a Hydroworx pool and you see them walking painlessly and getting exercise in an environment that can help change their lives. That's a very visual thing and a vision that brings pleasure and hope. That's the visual you have when you think of Hydroworx pools: not some amorphous amount of money, but a vision of working to change those people's lives.

And there are other stories, other applications, too.

Alberto Salazar trained the US Olympic team, and in the ten thousand meter run, the athletes who trained using the Hydroworx pools won Olympic medals. Through using the pools, they cut down on the number of miles they had to put in running outside, so it saved their joints while strengthening their muscles via water resistance. They were able to perform at a very high level because of the effects of water therapy training. In one picture I've seen, a medal winner is pointing to the crowd after the race finish. He was pointing to the people from Hydroworx, indicating their role in his success. It was the first medal the United States had won in this race in an incredibly long period of time, and he attributed it to Hydroworx.

And guess what? After the change of focus from money to this powerful, emotional and motivational story, the employee engagement in Hydroworx went *through the roof*.

What Hydroworx did was change their focus from a mess of numbers to a recognizable human story in which the company makes a difference.

It makes a huge difference because **suddenly everybody**

in the company understands their overall purpose, and feels good about being involved with it. In other words, when I say I want to do $25 million, you can understand that number, but what does that really mean? When I talk about individuals as patients who can be helped or athletes who can be trained to their best potential, I can connect to that. Everybody in that organization is now able to connect to that theme.

Many charitable organizations understand this concept. They have purpose-driven messages about helping people in Africa, or in the United States, to get a meal. They can really translate that to dollar donations because people understand that someone actually gets fed when they choose to help.

In Hydroworx, after the change from the dollar focus to the story-based message, people began to look at the individual patients rather than at the figures. The work had a human face on it that was different, beguiling, and easy to understand. The entire organization began to focus more on company culture: how they behave with each other and with the public, and those values they have. Then, great results followed.

Now it's true that the downturn in the economy really hurt them, as it's a very expensive product, and one that organizations have to consider for a while before buying. Nevertheless, they had a short time when revenue dipped, and after that, their bottom line shot up like a rocket. This pick-up in sales and morale is because of the vision they had for the organization.

In my opinion, Hydroworx Pools show the way forward for other companies and organizations. You may not sell therapeutic pools, but you can still look for the human story in your product or service. Once you've found it, you can spin it into a new viewpoint and focus for the company, one to share with the workforce at every level. Once this is done, greater engagement is sure to follow.

In this sense, this book is about strategic planning *with purpose.*

ABOUT ME

In the writing of this book, I've been asking for feedback from friends and colleagues on what facts and information to include in the manuscript. As a group, they've made it clear that it would be good to include a little information on who I am and where I've come from, with a focus on strategic planning. As one friend put it, "Who is this guy and why should we listen to him? If they don't know the answer, why *should* they listen to what you say?" So, here's a little autobiographical information with that in mind.

I grew up Pennsylvania, and then graduated with a BS in marketing at Penn State University. I then spent most of my subsequent career – over 30 years – in the radio business. I've owned and operated radio stations in Pennsylvania, New York, and Maryland, and sold them to Clear Channel Communications in 1998.

After that, I started a network syndicating talk shows at offices in New York City in the Empire State Building. I sold that to Salem Communications in 2002. All this gave me a lot of experience in communication, planning and dealing with different workforces.

STRATEGIC PLANNER AND COACH

I then looked around for a new challenge and these days, I work as a strategic planner. I have also been working regularly with CEOs and leadership teams as an executive coach. My role there is to work with senior teams, helping them develop their leadership skills, so they in turn can mentor and assist others. I want to help them make better decisions, become better leaders, produce better results and have purpose.

If I think about what I'm doing, I can translate it into "fives."

- The revenues of the companies that I work with, in total, are more than $5 billion. This is the big business end of town.

- The number of employees that these organizations have in total is over 5,000 people. With that many employees on the payroll, the CEOs have their work cut out to get and keep the level of engagement they want.

- I end up doing around 500 meetings a year, more than two a day. That can be either one-to-one meetings with CEOs, strategic planning sessions, or other coaching group meetings. Each session is scheduled one at a time and is very intimate.

I work with a broad spectrum of people – lots of different CEOs at any given moment. Currently I'm working with at least 60 CEOs, both here and abroad, and I do six or eight strategic planning engagements every year. I've done 50 or so strategic planning engagements over the past six or eight years.

VISTAGE

I'm also a chairman with a company called Vistage. Vistage is the largest CEO membership organization in the world. It's over 50 years old, having been founded in Wisconsin in 1957. It has over 17,000 members worldwide, and is active in 17 countries. It is a peer-to-peer organization for CEOs.

My affiliation with Vistage began a few years after I started my management consulting practice. Some of my clients were also Vistage members, and they suggested that I should become a Vistage chairman.

As a Vistage chairman, I facilitate a monthly meeting with each CEO group under my care. We talk about issues, decisions, and opportunities in an environment that's safe and nonthreatening. We ask and answer questions, seek advice, and give and receive mentoring. We have conversations that members might not feel comfortable having in any other place in the world. Every month I meet individually with each CEO with whom I've done strategic planning or individual coaching.

Most Chairs have one or two groups under their care, but I have four. I have two of the CEO groups, meaning there are larger companies in those groups. Groups generally run between 12 and 16 members. I also have the care of a small business group, and, finally, I have a key executive group. The small business group consists of companies with an entrepreneurial focus. The key executive groups are CFOs, chief selling officers, marketing people, and a variety of people who support or are on executive teams within those organizations.

All in all, I have in the range of 60 plus executives within the Vistage framework that I work with every month. I find this work fulfilling. Naturally, it is also time-consuming, and I take the time to plan my days quickly and efficiently. I not only teach *Fast Track Strategic Planning*, but I actively make use of it in my own life.

So, that's who I am: a busy guy who likes to live connected and who wants to help others connect through human stories. In my view, efficiency and humanity do go hand in hand.

ASKING FOR MONEY IS STAGE 3.

WE'RE STILL AT STAGE 2!

Section Two

What is Strategic Planning?

STRATEGIC PLANNING DEFINED

Strategic planning is a process whereby an organization looks at opportunities in the market place and decides through that process where they're going and how they're going to get there. In other words, it's a plan with a purpose, using strategy rather than trusting to blind luck.

My version of *Fast Track Strategic Planning* is a little different from other strategic planning programs, because it is, as it says, *fast track*.

Normally, the strategic planning process involves many people and takes months to finish. In the fast track process, the aim is to deliver a plan within forty-eight hours that will get you 80% of the way in less than 20% of the time.

There are a number of advantages to having the job done so quickly.

- Your people will be less tired than they'd be from sitting in meetings for weeks or months. Their minds will be fresher and better focused.

- You'll be able to implement the completed plan much faster, which is an advantage when situations change so quickly in business. A plan that is months in the making might be obsolete by the time it's completed, let alone implemented.

I believe organizations need to have a plan they can execute sooner rather than later. Today the velocity of marketplace change is greater than ever before. If you take six months to complete a plan, the market might have changed in the interim. There are lots of examples of new products or services that are outdated within six months of being brought into the market.

In today's world, you need a plan that is functional, helping you run your business, and helping you focus on the right types of things. You need a plan that's a living, breathing document you can change on the fly.

So, how does Fast Track differ from the strategic planning model taught to MBA candidates?

In *Fast Track Strategic Planning*, we use everyday language to explain things. The pictures we paint of the initiatives, the goals and the vision of the company are told in human-centered *stories*. We strive for absolute clarity. When you think about translating your strategic plan to an entire organization, you want everybody in that organization to be able to understand it. That means it shouldn't be filled with acronyms and jargons that nobody except a few people can understand.

TALKING IN STORIES

When we talk about the vision of an organization, we could talk about having a return on investment equal to ten percent of net income, an employee engagement ratio of X percent or a net promoter score of X or Y.

All these things are a legitimate part of a plan, but what do they mean to the people at the frontline of the organization? In *Fast Track Strategic Planning*, we talk about stories that show the impact our company has on customers and what that might mean in real world terms.

MORE OF THE HYDROWORX STORY

Let me give you an example. Remember the story of Hydroworx in Part One? It's the company which sells therapeutic pools to various institutions. They're expensive. They have treadmills in them. They are used to train professional athletes, and to rehabilitate people who've had hip, knee, and other joint replacements, as well as others suffering from a variety of conditions and ailments that make normal weight-bearing exercise difficult or impossible. They allow exercise and training in an almost-weightless environment, so suddenly people who could not exercise much at all can do so easily. These Hydroworx pools are all over the country. Probably every major sport in the USA, such as soccer, football, and track, uses these pools.

If you remember, the company vision was changed and the engagement went way up. It is now *not* about having revenue of X dollars, or even striving for a certain percentage market share. It was too hard to gain full employee engagement that way. Instead, the company vision is to **change the lives of fifty thousand patients**. It's not about acronyms or market share or dollar amounts. It's all about the story. Having a human-based story as a vision statement is a more solidly real world way of thinking about it and it promotes enthusiastic and emotional engagement.

A VALVES STORY

Let me give you a second example. I work with another company that makes valves, which, on the surface, are admittedly a very non-sexy product.

Imagine the following conversation between two people.

"What do you do?" asks the first person.

The second replies, "We make valves."

"Oh."

Now, this company had their annual town hall meeting. Before the CEO came in they were flashing pictures of these valves on the screen. I'm sure everybody was very proud of those valves. Then in walked the CEO and everybody went quiet.

And this is what he said: "This morning at 7 o'clock, a janitor walked into the basement of a school in Vermont and turned fifteen of our valves so that kids could be warm and safe while they were in school. At 9 o'clock this morning, they turned 40 valves in an operating room in Minneapolis, and we helped save three lives today. And you thought we just sell valves."

Defining that purpose in a different, human-centered way means getting across the vision of what you are as an organization in a way that has real meaning for people. Suddenly valves are no longer "just valves." They're part of the human story, part of the story of health and education of the country's children.

FAST TRACK STRATEGIC PLANNING

ON FREQUENCY

In the climate of this modern world, strategic planning should be *continuous*. It's always forward-facing, and that is the clear difference between, let's say, a strategic plan and a budget. Most budget processes look *back* at historic data to see what was spent and how it was spent. Budgets are part of a strategic plan, but they're a historic view of what you spent in the past and what you hope to spend in the future and how you plan to be financially secure and meet strategic objectives.

- Budgets **look back** and try to forecast what might happen in the future.

- Strategic plans **look forward** and make a conscious path to what might happen in future.

From a strategic standpoint, there are key initiatives that are the genesis of a budget. Out of those initiatives come the elements that form the budget.

You need to check on whether you're actually achieving these strategic initiatives on an *ongoing basis*. Your strategic plan should be a living, breathing document. It should never just sit on the shelf and gather dust, which a lot of strategic plans do. **Your strategic plan is something that should be pulled out, reviewed and examined, at minimum, every quarter**.

It should be recognized and read and retold to *every* employee in the organization. That way, everybody from the ground up understands their role in the plan – instead of having some guys who sit in the high corner office, making a plan that they then funnel down to all of us, expecting us to execute it. Understanding a role in a plan means understanding what is being done, why it is being done, and who is responsible for doing it. Everybody has to play an active and well-defined role in this.

ON STRATEGY

We've talked about the <u>fast</u> aspect of *Fast Track Strategic Planning* - which means the plan is done in 48 hours. What about the *strategic* part? Where does that come in?

Strategy has to do with key elements of a plan. **Strategy** is *how* you plan to get from here to there, and how you plan to achieve the results you aim for.

Let's look at an example based on travel. (Remember my cheap friends who take twelve-hour flights when I'd rather take a three-hour flight?) In this example, let's say we want to go from Pennsylvania clear across the country to Hollywood on the west coast. There are certain choices we would have to make to work out a strategy to get from point A to point B:

- Do you travel from A to B in a plane, a car or a train?

- Do you take a northern route or a southern route?

- What kinds of things do you want to see along the way?

As you see from this example, key elements of strategy are those things that help you decide *how* you're going to take that trip. You weigh benefits and pros and cons. Of course not everyone who makes a strategic plan is going to come up with the same one, because different people have different priorities. Remember my cheap friends who take twelve-hour flights? They think the pros of saving money and using air mile points on travel outweigh the cons of spending a lot more time on the trip. In my case, I think the time saved is worth more to me than the extra outlay of money. We both plan according to our priorities.

THE HOLLYWOOD STORY

Let's say, for example, that you have a vision of going to Hollywood, California.

You have a **vision** of what Hollywood means, and what it will be like when you get there.

Here's part of that vision. When you go to Hollywood:

- There's the famous Hollywood sign you should see to verify that you're there.

- There are going to be palm trees.

- There are people driving around on the 405 freeway with their tops down. They'll be wearing dark glasses and the wind will be blowing through their hair.

- There is the Pacific Ocean and the Venice Beach boardwalk.

By these signs, you know you've arrived in Hollywood. These are the clues that let you say with certainty, "Okay, now I'm in Hollywood."

That's the vision, and the overall goal. That's the place

you aim to be, with all the experience tied up in that place.

Then the **strategic** elements kick in and you start to plan. Again, these strategic decisions focus on *how* you're going to get from where you are to Hollywood. You'll need to answer questions like:

- What mode of transportation will we use?

- What route will we take?

- What do we want to see along the way?

- How long do we want to take on the journey?

- How much are we prepared to spend on this trip?

In business, the elements of a **strategic plan** often include things like these:

- Is there technology we want to employ that will give us advantage over a competitor in the same field?

- Is there a geographic region we're going to expand into when we get the opportunity?

- What are the advantages of expanding into that region?

- Are there people or processes that we need to access to make the difference?

- Do we want to grow or are we satisfied to stay the size we are? What level of profit is desired?

- What growth is there available in our field?

- If we're manufacturing, are there new products or new raw materials we may need that may change the entire way we do business?

- Are there circumstances that have come into play that might change the way we do business?

- Are there services that we can offer that are unique to our company?

- Are there market forces that have come into play that might change the way we do business?

- What does a 'win' look like?

These are the concepts you have to think about from a strategic standpoint that allow you to get a little further down the road.

ON TIME SPAN

Unlike most budgets or most plans that people have that are shorter in span, a *Fast Track Strategic Plan* is focused solely on the next three to five years from where you are today. It includes a vision of what you'd like to see for this organization. There are key strategic elements you have to employ to get to that point and therefore, you know you want to be on the right road, and you need checkpoints along the way.

Back in our example: If you're going to Hollywood and you get off the road for a detour, or you took a wrong turn, then to get back on, you have to have some place to point at to say, "This where we *should* be according to the plan." So you want to find the right route to get back on the plan.

That's what a strategic plan does. **A good strategic plan aligns everybody in the organization behind some key initiatives that are translatable to everybody**. That way everyone can say, "That's my focus. This is how I'm going to get there. This is my role in the strategic plan for this organization."

ON TACTICS

So what is the difference between strategy and tactics?

Back in our Hollywood example, a *strategy* is that we're going to take the northern route. Another strategy would be to travel by car, or by plane, or by taking a train.

The *tactics* are smaller things like how many miles you're planning to drive every day. The planned tactic might be that you're going to drive eight hours a day, averaging sixty miles an hour. By implementing these tactics, you can work out that you should be able to drive between four and five hundred miles a day. That means you can get from Pennsylvania to Ohio by the first night. By the second night you're going to get from Ohio to St. Louis. You can preplan where you should be at any given point in the journey.

Additionally, tactics may include where and when you stop and have dinner, because that could affect the time it will take and the quality of the meal. The time you stop could affect how hungry you will be, and even how long you'll need to wait for a free table. In the tactics for this trip, you plan the places you're going to stop and eat, get gas, spend the night, and take any other necessary or advisable pause.

In business, therefore, **the tactics are the way you execute on the big strategic ideas**. Let's say that you're going to invest in a new technology that will help you in your business. *That's* a strategy. You weigh the cost of the investment against the forecast benefits. If you're going to institute an ERP (Enterprise Resource Planning) system in an organization, it's a large technological change that impacts every aspect of that organization. That's a big *strategic initiative*.

Underneath that, there's the question of how all of the departments will utilize and implement that large strategic idea. Those are the *tactics*.

A BUSINESS EXPANSION STORY

For example, what if you wanted to grow your business to a larger geographic footprint within a certain period?

Let's say your business is headquartered in the eastern half of the United States and you'd like to look at the entire country and expand that footprint to give you greater access to sales, and therefore a bigger market share and a bigger national impact. That's a large *strategic initiative*.

The tactics under that strategic initiative are these:

- How are we going to do that?

- Do we need a plant in a particular region?

- If so, which region would be best?

- Do we need sales teams in the western half of the United States?

All of those tactics help accomplish the larger strategic goal, and they can trickle down as far as you want in the organization.

Ultimately, tactics are the elements that allow the larger strategic goal to happen.

STRATEGIC VS. BUSINESS PLANNING

Strategic plans are *forward-facing*. They're always looking to the future, with a goal and a plan for reaching that goal.

Business plans have a tendency to be shorter, and to focus on metrics of performance and the tactics required to reach shorter term goals.

For example, business plans focus on monthly financial statements. They aren't generally predictors of future outcomes. They're indicators, but they're not predictors. A lot has to do with the timespan of the plan, but also with looking at the plan in terms of focusing on the key strategic initiatives. A business plan is what you're going to do for the next ninety days. A strategic plan is where you're going to be in five years and how you're going to get there.

So, let's jump in to the practical details of the *Fast Track Strategic Planning* process.

Section Three

Practical Matters

THE KEY COMPONENTS

One of the key differences between the *Fast Track Strategic Planning* process and other, longer processes is that it all boils down to a single page. That's right – a single page! This is a single-sided page with normal sized text. It's something that can be read in a couple of minutes and easily understood. It can be held in your mind without having to take a lot of notes as you read.

THE SINGLE PAGE

There's a reason for fitting this into a single page. **If you can't deliver the plan in a single page, it's too damn big for anybody to understand**. There are too many elements that are not critical that are not going to get to everybody in the organization.

The outcome of the *Fast Track Strategic Planning* process is to have a single page plan that talks about

- your vision,

- your purpose,

- what you currently do as an organization,

- large strategic initiatives,

- and the elements of defining what that vision looks like when you've arrived.

It will also include :

- The key core values and guiding principles of the organization, which are the defining DNA of the organization. These describe how people should behave for the organization to be the best it can be. It explains how we behave with people, internal and external, at the highest and lowest levels of the organization.

- It sets the tone for the company culture.

So what, exactly, does the *Fast Track Strategic Planning*

process give you? Why is it better than any other form of planning?

Any organization that initiates a fast track plan and carries it forward gets the following products:

1. A **single page** of easily-read, easily-digested directions.

2. **Supplemental pages** to support each element of the plan. Thus, each major statement or supposition in the plan will have some expanded information which can be accessed when needed.

The key elements of the plan are as follows:

• There's a **vision,** which concerns the future point in time that we're moving toward. It's where you're going, why we're going there, and in addition to that, what it looks like along the way and when you arrive. It's not just some words put together in a hurry; it's a word picture that fully illustrates the where, why, how, and what.

- There are **core values** for the plan and the organization, which are non-negotiable. These core values are the three or four key things which describe this organization's behaviors and culture. These core values are like the center line in a highway. They're the three or four things from which you don't deviate. These are elements that are essential to the organization, that represent it at its brightest and best.

- On either side of that, since people are imperfect and come from different places and with different values, there are **guiding principles** that give you a little bit more room to maneuver along the way.

- I would liken the guiding principle to the rumble strips on either side of the highway where if you go too far to the right or too far to the left, you get a rumble. It warns you you're in danger of running off the road, and it makes you come back towards the center. Those are the things that help guide the organization in decisions like hiring and firing. Key decisions regarding personnel, future of the organization, and issues with vendors are all driven by the values of the organization. Those should all be explained in words that all people in the organization can understand.

- A construction business I work with provides a great example of a guiding principle or a core value. We tried at first to use polite language, but these are construction guys on work sites, so we ultimately discovered that one of their core values could only be expressed as 'no assholes or prima-donnas allowed.' They understood precisely what that meant. This was written into the strategic plan's core values with them in mind. The company is pretty proud that they used those words because they have an impact on their employees. If you have an asshole or a prima-donna at a construction work site, that person doesn't have your back, and you can get hurt. Many times in this kind of hazardous job, people get injured because someone is trying to either show off or be something they're not. The construction guys didn't want any of that.

- **Strategy Statement**. This defines the one thing that must be done extraordinarily well to achieve the vision. What should the driving force be, and how does this differ from what we're doing now?

- **Strategic anchors**. These are those key elements that you do well now as a company. It's a nonlinear process, looking at defining what you already do well and breaking it into three or four major buckets. Most organizations really fall into two to four areas that they feel good about in terms of things that they do. As the saying goes, "If it ain't broke, don't fix it," so these strategic anchors are important.

- **Strategic initiatives**. These are the big goals, the big initiatives that will help you get to that vision of the place you want to be. They are the way you go from who you are today to who you're going to be in the future.

- **Action steps.** The action steps are the things you do to help achieve those strategic initiatives. Action steps are broken down by key department, division, and individuals. They explain who does what, when do they do it, and what are the sub-goals that will help them accomplish the larger goal. Sub-goals are valuable along the way because they help make visible and measureable progress.

- **Strategic dashboards**. These are not key performance indicators for individuals. Strategic dashboards are about looking at the big strategic initiatives and measuring how you're performing on those. It helps you see where more work needs doing and where the sub-goals are being met.

- **What matters most**. What is the most important thing you should do next? Once you're through the plan, what's the most important thing that you can do to take the next steps to your ultimate goal?

- **Prioritizing.** This is about prioritizing things that'll have the greatest impact on the business, given the time, money, resources, and people that you have. You want to get some quick wins. You want people to feel they're making progress towards larger goals via the meeting of the sub-goals.

- **Execution plan.** This means you take all those pieces, and you say, how are we going to roll this out? How frequently are we going to meet? And how are we going to measure what we're doing through the dashboard?

Everyone in the organization should know about the plan and their role, and the expected steps, goals and sub-goals. If they don't know what they are supposed to be doing and when, then nothing happens.

SUMMARY

A fast track strategic plan is a single piece of paper with eight components. It will be supported by attached documents that provide the detail of all those things.

1. Vision

2. Core values and guiding principles

3. Strategic anchors

4. Strategic initiatives

5. Action steps

6. Dashboards

7. Quick wins or what matters most

8. Execution plan

Let's have a closer look at those eight pieces one by one. Understanding these brings you a long way to producing a solid and workable plan.

1. VISION

The first part of the *Fast Track Strategic Planning* process is vision.

I will start with what visions traditionally sound like. That way I can tell you what you *shouldn't* be doing. Here is a traditional expression of a business vision.

"My company is the biggest world class distributor of product X in the eastern half of the United States, achieving a net income or customer satisfaction level of X or Y. We are recognized as the leader in our industry in this area."

On one level, this sounds pretty good. It makes sense to have clear targets. Unfortunately, however, this vision is lacking in *purpose.*

Secondly, I would defy anybody to repeat that. After all, you would like your company vision to be something that is on the lips of every employee. If you ask them about the company vision, they need to be able to explain it back to you.

What I try to encourage people to do is to distill this information to the essence of what it is you really want to *be.* Not X, Y, percentages and net distribution. **Your vision should express what you want to be and to do in** *human story terms*. Remember the Hydroworx pools that help patients and athletes every day? Remember the valve manufacturer that makes it possible for children to learn in a comfortable environment and for patients to receive effective and often life-saving medical treatment?

So, you distill the information in human terms. Your vision is what you really, really want to *be*.

If you happened to be a potato farmer, what you want to do is to feed the world healthy food at a reasonable price, so that people can grow up and live productive lives. You want to do this while maintaining your business in the best social and economic health possible.

The ideal vision is a word picture that probably shouldn't exceed 15 words. It should distill what you do down to a core statement.

An example of a people-centered vision comes from an insurance company client of mine. The vision for the insurance company was about making sure that everybody's life was safe, that nobody was hurt and that no business was lost that could not be repaired. It comes back to the story. Thus their core 15 word vision might be: **Our safety net is so big that no one falls through the mesh.**

Another example is from a construction company client

of mine. They believed their future state was to have highly motivated and engaged employees at every level in the organization, who delivered customer service that was branded as *their* level of customer service, not just good service. Or, in the short 15 word core vision, **Our highly engaged employees build extraordinary places where people love to live, work and play.**

The case of Toms Shoes is a great example of a company with human story and purpose. Toms is a company that sells wonderful shoes. It was founded in 2006 in California and is a for-profit company that operates a non-profit subsidiary. Toms shoes are environmentally friendly and smart but casual. The Toms model of business is that from day one, every time you buy a pair of Toms shoes, the Toms company gives a pair of shoes away to someone in need. So, integrated into the very fabric of this business is a very day-to-day, moment-to-moment philanthropic model. This aspect of the company is built firmly into the vision and has been there from the beginning.

As you can imagine, the level of employee engagement at Toms is super high. Not only do the company employees and management at every level feel good about the vision, but customers who buy the shoes feel equally good about helping a worthwhile cause *and* getting a killer pair of shoes at the same time.

VISION STRUCTURE

So, let's recap the important aspects of *Vision*:

- Vision is a **word picture** with the emphasis on human story.

- It is **15 words or less,** so it can be quoted and understood after hearing it once.

- It describes **a future scenario** in terms of positive, human-based outcomes.

- It is **story-oriented** with characters – the people you are benefiting in most cases.

- In an ideal world it may well incorporate something **more purposeful;** e.g. the vision for Toms Shoes is probably something like: **To give away one pair to the needy every time we sell a single pair,** which incorporates purpose.

- Ideally it **feeds back,** so not only does the vision raise engagement at every level of the organization, but it also raises engagement in consumers who feel good about their association with this positive-vision organization.

The vision statement as it stands alone is about 15 words and then underneath that you can say: We'll know we've arrived at our destination *when* ... these certain elements happen. Then you **add three or four bullet points.** One should be a financial bullet point because everyone has a different measure of a number they use as bottom line.

The other bullet points could include things like:

- We are a place where people love to come to work every day;

- Leaders abound at every level and succession plans are in place;

- Customers and vendors recognize our impact and we are their preferred vendor;

Additionally, you could include development plans that you've instituted. A development plan might say that every person is getting better at their job every day. This should be measureable with better engagement, more work and going the extra mile as pointers.

If I am sitting with my team working on this, rather than judging good or bad elements about the company, I would have everybody write down a series of five words that they believe are meaningful to them and that also describe what they think the company should look like in the future. This is about what would make this company perfect in the future.

We can then gather those words together. These words can then be put in categories. When you have them in categories then you begin to put them in a sentence.

When you find a sentence you then write that sentence, and you see how that fits and you let it sit there for a while. Then after a while you come back and you adjust that sentence until it really is exactly what you mean. You will be surprised at really what comes out when you focus and set out to say *we are this*, and *the company is this,* and *when this happens the company will be perfect.*

Here's an example from a law firm. I was in the room with three people. These three people started to write down five words or phrases designed to express the perfect state of this business in the future.

Here are some of the results.

- Engagement

- Love to work here

- Culture

- Search us out

- Financial

- Value

We ended up with a vision that said, "We are recognized for delivering value driven outcomes for clients while being a great place to practice law and work. Culture is the engine that drives our growth."

VISION EXERCISE

To begin the *Fast Track Strategic* process, you'll need to assemble your planning team for a full day meeting. While you can certainly hold these sessions in an office boardroom, it's often good to get out of the building and find a more creative environment. It's also good to be away from any possible distractions, such as phone calls and emails.

During the course of Section Three, we'll break down this day into different exercises. We'll also suggest an hour by hour schedule.

DAY 01 / HOUR 01 / VISION

Begin by have your planning team members each write a short story (one paragraph) about where they see the company in the future. Make sure they exclude specific numbers and finances. Ask them to be creative and to paint word pictures.

Once they're done, have them present their visions to the group.

As they present their vision, similarities will emerge and you can use these to prepare a powerful word picture (vision) for your company.

DAY 01 / HOUR 02 / THE 5 WHY'S

A simple, powerful exercise to get at purpose is The 5 Why's.

Break your planning group into teams of three or four. Start with a statement which describes what your company does: we sell X or we offer X services. Ask "Why" this is important five times.

As you get to the 5th why, you'll find you are at the fundamental purpose of your company.

2. CORE VALUES AND GUIDING PRINCIPLES

CORE VALUES

Core values are those non-negotiable values that represent the DNA that is apparent to everybody in an organization. They describe how we behave.

When you walk into a business's front door, you get a feel for that business within *moments*. Many times the company values jump out at you immediately. It's in the way you are greeted at the front desk, the way the place looks, the maintenance, the color scheme, the smell, the way people move; it's reflected in every aspect of their being.

Those **core values** are the three or four value elements that represent those things that are core to the organization. These are positive things that everybody there recognizes as being already in play. They're not aspirational values, they're not occasional values, they're constants; they're the guiding principles, the things that make that organization *go*. The core values are the things that lift it from "mediocre" to "good" or even to "great."

What I try to do with each one of these core values is to ask everybody in the group to tell me what they believe. I generally get a wide variety of answers. Even if somebody has already written down and distributed a list of core values to them, it is likely they haven't thought about them carefully in some time, which is a pretty sad thing.

Having gathered a large, varied group of values, we either try to narrow that down or else we define (or redefine) what is really meaningful to the organization in language that is appropriate. (Remember those construction-worker guys with their "no assholes or prima-donnas"? That is appropriate for the construction industry. That would not be appropriate for a menswear outfitter.)

Good core values examples might be:

- Safety first—no one gets hurt.

- We jump through hoops for our clients.

- Trust—we have each others back.

- We're on the job from beginning to end.

- We are accountable and own every problem.

- We're on time, every time.

- We deliver more than expected.

- We act as one team.

- We treasure each relationship and work to deliver extraordinary outcomes.

GUIDING PRINCIPLES

Core values are three or four in number for each company or organization. Guiding principles can be up to ten or twelve.

Guiding principles reinforce the core values but they give people some leeway to move a little bit to the right or the left, which further defines the core values. In other words, a guiding principle takes a core value and expands on it a lot more.

If you think of your company, your core values are those elements that are not negotiable. The guiding principles are those things that define you as a person at the company.

In other words, what does it mean to be a person working for this company? What does that really stand for? What's the code of behavior that defines me as a person? The answers define the culture of the organization: interaction, behavior and a variety of things that enhance those core values that you currently have.

I like to build a PowerPoint presentation to show each one of these guiding principles. Say a company's core values are: Integrity, Respect, Teamwork, Quality and Innovation. The guiding principles for being a team member of this company are:

- Being honest and trustworthy—our word is our bond

- We are focused on extraordinary service and always "happy to help"

- Being resourceful, innovative and ready to "roll up my sleeves" to get the job done

- Welcoming accountability to each other and to our mission

- Being deeply dissatisfied with the status quo; passionately driven for what could be

- Embracing conflict in the pursuit of excellence and the best outcomes for all stakeholders

- Being held to the higher calling of our core values

- Contributing to a culture that is fun, challenging and an environment where we grow and learn

- Striving to become an expert without boundaries

- Being eager to own any customer request, seeing it all the way through to resolution

All of these things could be guiding principles for an organization. All of these things help reinforce and implement the core values. All of these things help keep the organization's community culture positive.

A CULTURE ARTIFACT

I sometimes work with companies that have strong values, which show up in artifacts and rituals steeped in culture. They believe that their values drive every aspect of their organization and keep them strong.

One of these companies has a core value of elegance.

The owner of this enterprise is a wonderful, worldly gentleman. He and his brother started out many years ago in the real estate business. They then moved to London, an international poster city for elegance. They had little capital to spare, but they made a decision that elegance was to be one of their core values. Elegance became *non-negotiable*.

With this in mind, they went and bought suits on Savile Row, a street in Mayfair specializing in bespoke tailoring for men. The term *Savile Row* has become synonymous with elegant quality in men's attire. This executive laid out some of his small capital on a dark suit with dark shoes and a black briefcase. To this day, all executives in that company still wear dark shoes, dark suits and have dark briefcases.

They take care to be impeccable that every word they send out of the organization represents the elegance that they want to have going forward unbroken into the future. This core value is foremost in their minds. Of course, with a core value like that, it's driving a lot of specific and elegant behavior in the organization. It is very important to this organization to be on point with purpose, and to be on point with values because without them they'd feel totally adrift.

THE NARNIA STORY

Another story that illustrates this principle comes from *The Chronicles of Narnia* by C.S. Lewis.

In the first book in the series, *The Lion, the Witch and the Wardrobe,* Aslan the Lion allowed himself to be captured by the White Witch. Aslan was the leader representing Jesus Christ in this book, and was offered up as a sacrifice for the life of a young boy, Edmund, who had become a traitor to Aslan's cause. The White Witch took Aslan to a stone table on top of the hill and performed a ritual killing by binding him up and stabbing him with a special knife.

After that was done the sun came up. Edmund's two sisters, Susan and Lucy see some friendly mice nibbling

I DIDN'T THINK THIS WAS
WHAT YOU MEANT
WHEN YOU CALLED ME
THE ANCHOR!

the ropes that bind Aslan's body. The girls look up and suddenly Aslan is up and bounding around. He is alive! They discover the witch didn't know the rules, which were *deeper and more valuable* rules that existed from the beginning of time. These rules said a willing sacrifice could turn back death.

That is really the rules we are talking about: core values are rules that are so meaningful that they never change. Values can't change for an organization, especially core values.

If they do change, that may be because your company has been sold, or you have had a dramatic change in leadership or direction, which brings a different set of values to the organization. If the values replaced were closely held values that the organization has held for some time, it will be extremely disruptive. In fact, it can be destructive. The organization will no longer feel like the same organization. It may need another name or a different sense of purpose.

Not all organizations are value-driven. Some of them use their stated values just for show. In my opinion, core values are an essential part of the *Fast Track Strategic Planning* process. It is important that the values are based on somewhere the company really wants to live and are not all about lip-service.

VALUES AND PRINCIPLES EXERCISE

While you can hold these meetings separately, I like to do as much as possible in a single session. With that in mind, arrange for your planning team to meet once more.

DAY 01 / HOUR 03 / CULTURE DIG

An exercise to identify and establish core values and guiding principles is to do a "Culture Dig." Through this you can identify those values that are central to your organization. Break your planning team into groups of three or four. Have them look around your company for:

- Artifacts and symbols—logos, titles, parking assignments, language used

- Stories—heroes/heroines, successes/failures, hirings/firings

- Relationships—subcultures, networks, reporting relationships

- Rituals & Rules—dress codes, validation, performance metrics, formal gatherings

Have them report back using words and comments that describe the culture they found.

3. STRATEGIC ANCHORS

The third piece of the *Fast Track Strategic Planning* process is **strategic anchors**.

Often companies don't know what they do really well. Sometimes they have a lot of things they do pretty well, but have never really looked at these in detail. To draw these out, here is a nonlinear process where I draw what I call a *strategic amoeba*. This comes from Patrick Lencioni's book *The Advantage,* so we give him full credit on this. It's a simple way to look at SWOT (strengths, weaknesses, opportunities, threats) and competitive advantage.

You draw an amoeba, and you ask the members of the team to throw words up to you that describe :

1. How they make decisions in a purposeful and unique way that allows them to maximize their success and differentiates them from competitors

2. How will they succeed?

3. What do they do well?

4. Simple truths about their business

These could be customer service, many locations, convenient locations, great staff, training, whatever it would happen to be. Then we walk through a process where we tire everybody out doing that and it can last a while because I have filled up a big white board with many different thoughts. Is there something else you do? What about this, what about that?

Once that is done you take a break, and then you come back and you try to connect all these things into areas that are key filters to inform other decisions. Usually these rough ideas can be grouped into areas like people, profit and process. Those groupings become your strategic anchors.

Strategic anchors are different for each organization, but it's always a conversation about what you do, and placing the higher priority items in bigger buckets. If you think about what you need to change or add or delete to get to the next level, you have to say, "These are our biggest advantages. How do we get to the next level? These are the things we suggest."

Once you have your strategic anchors you use them to drive all other decisions. An example would be having a strategic anchor featuring people. The organization would need to place an emphasis on talent acquisition, development, clarity of vision, goals and chain of command – as well as identifying high-potential performers, including rewards and compensation, within a culture that's rich in feedback.

ANCHORS EXERCISE

DAY 01 / HOUR 06 / DEEP ANCHORS

The deep anchor exercise is designed to help you explore the deep anchors that lie under your business.

Ask your planning team to answer these questions:

1. What is our brand promise?

2. What is the customer "problem" that we solve for the customer which NO ONE else solves?

3. What niche(s) do we or will we dominate?

4. Who is our ideal customer?

5. Which offers result in domination?

Once your team answers these questions in a breakout session, go back and complete your strategic amoeba exercises.

Once you've finished this exercise, you'll have finished the first day of the *Fast Track Strategic Planning* process.

4. STRATEGIC INITIATIVES

The fourth piece of the *Fast Track Strategic Planning* process is **Strategic Initiatives**.

There are 10 different strategic initiatives that you may decide are going to propel your organization forward toward your vision. Not all of them would be appropriate to every organization because some are company-specific.

Here's a quick list before we go into further detail –

1. Growth/size

2. Technology

3. Sales methods

4. Pricing/return/profit

5. New products/services

6. People/culture

7. Production capability

8. Natural resources

9. Distribution method

10. Geographic footprint

Let's go into detail in each of these areas.

One common strategic initiative is **growth**. You could say, "There is a certain level of revenue growth in the company now. I want to increase growth by 10%." This could be growing the number of customers, or it could be growth in terms of pure dollars. It could be growth in bottom line, or growth in members of the organization, or businesses in a franchise.

Another good example is **technology**, especially since new technology is forever changing the marketplace. Technology and its implementation as a strategic initiative can be very impactful.

Another common strategic initiative is sales channels, or **sales process**. In other words, you might currently have your own sales team, but then you want to go through brokers or a manufacturers' rep. You might also look at inside versus an outside solo team. This process determines how you reach out to your customers.

Pricing comes up as a strategic initiative from time to time. Your pricing strategy impacts how you go to market and directly impacts margin and profit.

It might be a **new line of products** or the reintroduction of a former product. Most US companies are products and services organizations. New products or services offered are key initiatives if this is your strategy.

It could be **people/culture**. No planning process should be without an initiative that relates to culture and people. Talent acquisitions and development should be part of the strategic plan. It is the big elephant in the room today. If you are not on the lookout for bright new talent, you are not going to grow your company – no matter what. Acquiring talent, keeping talent, growing talent, recognizing people and using personnel to their best advantage: That's where culture and strategy mesh.

Production capability speaks to the efficiency of your processes. If you are a manufacturing firm or a service provider delivering your product or service with greater speed, quality or quantity is key.

The price of **natural resources** can change margins, profits and markets. An example would be: as gold prices spiked, people flocked to companies buying old jewelry. Now that the price is down, that market has dried up. Natural resources can impact your strategy.

The way your products reach your customer, or **method of distribution** is another strategic area. Opening a warehouse across the country to reduce distribution and delivery costs is clearly a strategy.

Geographic footprint refers to what market(s) you serve. Answering the question will define resource allocation and a specific Plan of Action.

All of these strategic initiative areas are important to most organizations.

A strategic initiative is a high level goal that would alter the current course of the company as you drive it towards the vision. And for each strategic initiative, there must be something tangible that you would be able to see as a result.

TWO QUICK CAVEATS

I have found several pitfalls to look out for when it comes to strategic initiatives. Organizations should only undertake initiatives that they are ready, willing and able to execute on.

One pitfall is that if we are looking at a multi-year plan, which is what I would encourage people to do, they often try to accomplish all strategic initiatives in **their first 90 days**. In other words, they try to pack a great amount of achievement into a very small period of time, often without taking the necessary foundation steps on which to build those achievements. When they don't achieve everything on their list, they feel frustrated and quit.

The second pitfall is that they end up having **too many** strategic initiatives. When you get too many strategic initiatives, you're not focused enough on those that really matter, and again you don't accomplish anything. In most organizations, a laser focus ensures better results.

Another pitfall is that the **size and resources** of your organization must determine how many initiatives you can take on. This is because you can't take on more than you can accomplish in an organization. But regardless of the size of your organization, if you narrow the focus and try to accomplish a few big and truly important things in the prescribed time, you will end up executing at a higher level. So it is important as you look at your strategic initiatives to prioritize them over the period of time you are doing them as priorities may change over the year or from time to time.

In my experience, organizations traditionally have an appetite to really want to embrace this process. In other words, they really want to take on some big things and tick them off the list. They want to notch up the achievements. But when you look at their **readiness to be able to do it,** you discover either they don't have enough people, or they don't have the right people, or they don't have the correct resources for success.

An example might be that part of a company's strategic plan is to move the office to a brand new 80,000 square foot building. They want room to move, and they want to make an impression as a major player. They want the visible trappings of success. However, they have no resources to make the change. They are unwilling to figure out how to do it, so they are not able to do it. In other words, their strategic plan has no basis in reality and they really don't have the resources or the capabilities of putting together the resources to make it happen. So, it may not be a good initiative for this company to have. Even if they somehow put together the resources, these might be better used on a different initiative.

I would suggest narrowing your choice of strategic initiatives to the things that will have the **greatest impact** on your vision in your timeline because, these are living plans. Things happen so fast in business today that a decision that seems good now may not be a good decision or a good strategic initiative in 8-12 months. If that's the case, you need to go back frequently and say, "Are these initiatives still relevant? Are we on point? Is this really a valid way to look at this or not?" Your plan needs to change and evolve to take into account changes and evolution in the business environment.

INITIATIVES EXERCISE

Now it's time to gather your planning team for a second day of *Fast Track Strategic planning*. While we often hold these one after the other, it's not a problem to have a reasonable gap in between.

DAY 02 / PREPARATION

Ask each team member to complete a short survey and bring it to this session. The survey should read:

> Over the next four years, what are your four to six highest priorities that you believe will move your company from its present situation to its future vision?

> Each initiative must be expressed in the form of an outcome in the future. Please include why you believe this strategic initiative is core to reaching your vision.

Once each team member completes this process, you put all initiatives on a board and break them into strategic areas. Many might seem tactical or actually are tactical. The goal is to get these initiatives or goals into the largest strategic buckets possible.

5. ACTION STEPS

Action steps are the tactics to make your strategic initiatives real.

Under each strategic initiative, you'll need a series of sub-goals or **action steps** to take over the next three to five years, depending on how long you're planing for.

Remember, a good strategic plan has a goal or a vision no more than three to five years in the future, and which may be changed and evolved on a regular basis over time.

Each action step needs an individual owner or team who then takes emotional ownership. They will be the people who will really drive you to those goals, those big strategic initiatives. Each action step needs to have an owner, a deadline and method of reporting progress. Without these in place, nothing will be achieved.

These action steps are designed to drive the execution deeper in the organization so that everybody participates in achieving these big strategic initiatives. With full participation, you ensure everyone feels ownership/ responsibility and pride in progress.

Let's say I have four or five key initiatives I am working on at any time that are priorities for this organization. Now, the question is: How do I translate that into language that everyone understands, so they make a difference in us accomplishing this? How do I lay it out so that everyone understands their part in reaching our vision and helping us change the world?

As we've just said, the answer is to break each strategic initiative down into bite-sized action steps, then assign each action step to a person or team. That's how you connect the over-arching *why* to each person's day-to-day efforts.

ACTION STEPS EXERCISE

DAY 02 / HOUR 3 / ACTION STEP BREAKDOWN

Next, break your team down into smaller 3-4 person teams. Assign each team one key strategic initiative. Ask each team to identify one or two sub-goals (Action Steps) per year that will help meet the larger strategic objective and in turn propel the organization toward its vision.

Each team should identify these sub-goals, who will present the plan, and who will own these sub-goals. Once the sub-goals are established individual operating units and departments can establish goals that will support the larger goals and initiatives of the organization.

6. STRATEGIC DASHBOARDS

The sixth piece of the *Fast Track Strategic Planning* process is **strategic dashboards**.

A dashboard is a forward-facing look at the plan to answer questions like:

- How are we doing?

- Do we need to change?

- Do we need to look at things in a different light?

- Is this step or this part of the plan, put in place three years ago, still valid?

- What else has come into the market place that we didn't know about when this plan was created?

- Are there new factors that might have arisen that might change the way we approach going forward?

Every organization needs some sort of operational dashboard. This kind of dashboard might show things like:

- measures of efficiency,

- cash in the bank,

I FOUND THE CAKE, THE VENUE AND THE DRESS. IT WAS YOUR JOB TO FIND THE GROOM!

- profit and loss,

- customer satisfaction.

The dashboard might show different things that are intrinsic to the day-to-day running of the organization. All executives should be looking at them as the basis of their ongoing decisions. Everybody in the organization should have some key performance indicators operating at their level. A dashboard clearly identifies expectations for them. After all, if no one knows what they are meant to achieve, how do they know whether or not they are succeeding?

From a strategic standpoint, we need to look at a dashboard that prioritizes strategic initiatives and quickly gives you insight into your progress toward the larger goals. These need to be supported by strategic dashboards for departments and individuals. Everyone needs to be aligned and move toward the same goals and vision. Your strategic dashboard does not replace your operational dashboard. It keeps you focused on doing the right things to reach your vision.

THE DASHBOARD MEETING

I believe every organization should meet on a quarterly basis to determine whether or not it is on point, and what it needs to do next to gain or maintain progress.

During that **dashboard meeting,** you take a look at your dashboard and you ask questions like:

- Are we on point?

- Are we meeting the expectations we had with the plan?

- Are we actually executing it at a level that is necessary to make this plan go?

- Where are the gaps?

- Does this make a damn bit of difference to us or not at this point in time?

- What has changed in our organization? What has not changed ?

In other words, are we just doing stuff to do stuff, or are we doing stuff that is really meaningful and which will really bring about results? Ultimately, people want to do things that really have an impact on the organization.

So, at minimum, if you're working as an executive team together, and you want to produce the right results, you regularly need to spend time thinking and looking at the strategic plan and updating it. And you don't want the people in the organization to feel like the dirt-moving prisoners during World War II did in the Japanese prison camps. Let me explain!

THE WWII STORY

The story goes like this: During WWII, the Japanese guards made American prisoners move piles of dirt from one side of the yard to the other. The day after this they'd be made to move the piles of dirt back again. And so it went on, day after day.

After continually doing this, day in and day out, American prisoners would commit suicide by running away. It just drove them crazy because they had no purpose in what they were doing.

It would have been different if they'd been digging ground to produce crops, or even digging latrines. There would have been purpose in that. So what you don't want to do is ask your people in your organization to *move dirt*. You want them to feel there's purpose in their work and you want this to be true.

That's what your **dashboard meetings** are for. Those

FOLLOW THE PLAN, YOU NITWITS!

meetings are designed to ask and answer the question;:"Are we making progress towards our goal and is it still valid in our mind as an organization?"

You need to meet on a quarterly basis to look at the dashboard that aligns you with those strategic elements and issues that you're involved in. You need to make sure you're either on track or you're not, and decide how to act or react accordingly.

Every organization has a tendency to get off task, get busy and do things other than the strategic plan. And sometimes without a plan like this we have a tendency to do stuff that is not focused on the vision and the purpose of the organization and do stuff just to do *stuff*. It's busy work. It's moving dirt.

And so, make it a rule: there will be no moving dirt in your company. Make all work by all workers meaningful and purposeful by staying on point. The only way to do that is to come together and talk about it on a quarterly basis.

DASHBOARDS EXERCISE

DAY 02 / HOUR 05 / DASHBOARD

The next exercise is a dashboard exercise designed to gain alignment and establish priorities.

You begin by listing all of your high-level strategic initiatives. Next, ask each member to prioritize these initiatives by giving each initiative a number between 1 and 100. The total of the numbers assigned to each initiative cannot total more than 100.

This activity will allow you to determine how to prioritize initiatives. This, in turn, allows you to allocate resources to make sure they get done (on a prioritized basis.)

7. WHAT MATTERS MOST

The seventh piece of the *Fast Track Strategic Planning* process is **What Matters Most**.

After you've done all this work on this strategic plan, the real question is: How do you kick it off? In other words, how do you implement the plan in a way that will get it off to a rousing start? From our earlier example, this is what will give people the feeling they are actually on the road and heading toward Hollywood, California, and making progress.

You know when you take your kids in the car and they always ask, "Are we there yet? Are we there yet?" Everyone in your company is the same way when they think about the strategic plan. Everyone is anxious and wants to accomplish more than you might be able to do in a set timeframe.

So, now you need to **set priorities outlining what you can do in the next 72 hours,** in the next 30 days, in the next 3 months. Doing this says: *Here are some quick wins we can get so we feel like we'e winning and we're progressing.* You need to celebrate those wins. There's nothing that keeps people enthusiastically on point so much as demonstrating milestones that are being met on a regular basis.

You need to make sure something is happening all the

time so people know they are eating the whale one bite at a time, because with the big strategic initiatives it is very hard to see what is going to happen.

For example, expanding a company footprint by opening a new plant or putting a sales office in Georgia is a really big task. You have to hire people, who have to find a location in your preferred region. You have all these things you have to do before you can move on, and everybody needs to feel they are part of that process. Celebrating quick wins is one way to accomplish that, to create little bite sized things that you say, "Here's the first step, and that's going to the most meaningful thing to do to move forward today." It's determining what matters most, what will move us towards the vision quickest, and how can we set those key initiatives to move forward. It's about actively taking those steps when they're set. It's about creating momentum and seeing instant results.

WELL, ARE <u>YOU</u> GOING TO
TELL PHARAOH?

WHAT MATTERS MOST EXERCISE

DAY 02 / HOUR 06 / QUICK WINS

In the next exercise, we'll look for quick, immediate wins. Here's how you look for a win in the first 100 days.

Ask your team to propose a goal that has a sense of urgency. You're looking for a goal that needs to be accomplished in the short term. Decide which goal you will establish as your 100 day goal. Here are your steps to success:

- Focus on an important goal and give it a theme

- Define a measurable result

- Pinpoint accountability throughout your organization

- Drive innovation and experiment with new ways to work together

- Make learning deliberate

- Encourage careful planning and execution

8. EXECUTION PLAN

The last piece of the *Fast Track Strategic Planning* process is your **Execution Plan**.

At this stage, you want your *Fast Track Strategic Plan* to begin to cascade through the entire organization. You need everybody in the organization to be aware of the plan and those elements that are part of the plan so that they can understand what role they are playing in that overall plan. It has to cascade from the executive team to the supervisory level, to the line level, to the staff level, to the front lines. You need to have a plan to make that happen.

You might choose to hold a series of town hall meetings for regular interpretations of the plan. Some elements of the plan may need some more regular interpretation; for example, if you're a purpose-driven organization, you might need more than that. You might want to remind team members of that purpose every time you sit down and talk with two or more people present.

It's easy to tell one set of people and expect them to pass on the information, only to discover they didn't. Or maybe they put it in a memo hidden in a newsletter that never got read.

You have to talk about your plan until everybody gets it. Realizing that every single person in an organization has a relevant part to play in any progress doesn't come easily for most people.

THE TOWN HALL MEETING STORY

Let me give you an example. I was working with one particular CEO on a *Fast Track Strategic Plan*. Once we were done, his job was to communicate the plan to his high level sales people. Now, his top level sales people made upwards of $500,000 per year, and as a result, they had pretty big egos. These sorts of people tend to ignore information when it comes from anyone else, even their own CEO.

The CEO presented his case in an impassioned 30-40 minute presentation. He made four or five key points with respect to their ongoing direction in the company. These were his key people, remember – his high performers. They were demonstrably effective at their jobs.

When he left the room, however, the wheels began to fall off. Barely twenty minutes after he left the stage, I gave these high performers a quiz and asked them to write down what the four or five key points their CEO had given them were. Nobody could get more than *two* of these. And these were smart people! If this is an example of how much high performers retain, it makes you realize how little might be retained by those who are *not* at this level.

I like think of it like advertising or media, or even stage plays. You need to repeat things many times before people get it. The media version of this is "tell me three times." That is, in any script an important piece of information must be given a minimum of three times to make sure most people in the audience catch it.

And we have to remember that as executives, we're so attuned to what we're talking about that we've integrated it into our very being. After all, we planned it out in the beginning. We know it all, and we think everybody should get it the same way, and they *don't*. Clear and ongoing effort is required to have all of your people *really understand* the important key points.

This is where those fifteen word vision statements come in handy. These short, punchy stories are easy to remember. They're catchy. They're people-oriented. They're *story*. You know, a lot of people think if you put signs up on the wall, like, "Here's our vision," you're done. I don't think that's the case.

THE MONTHLY STORY

Here's another highly effective technique I call **Monthly Stories**.

What you do is ask a different team member each month, either an executive or someone at any other level, to interpret what one guiding principle or core value means to people *day to day*. This can be done either in writing or face to face, and can happen in team meetings or town hall meetings.

A lot of companies have town hall meetings, especially if they don't have to multiple locations all over the world. They take the time to interpret the core values of the organization by telling stories and citing people who are recognized for living those values. It's really easy to point out in individual one-on-ones how you're *not* doing well, but if you want to sell the *strengths* of the organization, you should be positive. Positive reinforcement is key to a productive and engaged workforce.

THE CASUAL MEMO

Another effective way I've found is to have the CEO take the initiative, and in a casual, informal way, update the company on big initiatives that are going on. This is not a structured, formal email. It is what's on your mind as the CEO working to keep your team in the loop. They might do this every other Friday with a little memo. It can show up in printed form on every desk, or you can email or text. As long as everyone gets it! It just keeps the priorities straight.

If you don't keep people in the loop, they'll perform their own actions and these might *not* be what you want them to do.

EXECUTION PLAN EXERCISE

DAY 02 / HOUR 07 / SCHEDULING

Have team members pull out their calendars. Put the following events on all executive calendars and make them non-negotiable:

- Quarterly off-site strategic planning events

- Town Hall meetings

- 1-2-1 feedback sessions with direct report employees

There you have it. If you follow these nine simple steps, you'll have your own *Fast Track Strategic Plan*.

Section Four

What Can Go Wrong?

There are several possible problems that stand in the way of the *Fast Track Strategic Planning* process.

- Cultural problems

- The wrong people in the room

- Lack of alignment

- No follow up

CULTURAL PROBLEMS

Sometimes we encounter cultural resistance in a company. This means that the people within the company set themselves *against* the plan, hoping to slow it down or stop it altogether. They usually do this because they perceive that your plan will change the culture from the way it has always been and they want everything to stay the same.

For example, a high tech firm that I know about hired similar people. Everyone wore black shirts, and had their fingernails painted black. As an unintentional cultural norm, they began to hire these avant-garde, really hipster people who were dressing like Goths. They didn't realize that's what they were doing; they just thought they were getting smart people. What happened is the culture became so narrow that they failed to be open to anybody else coming in. They became insular in outlook because there were no varied points of view. Then, when they tried to hire people outside of that narrow culture, the people who were there didn't like it. They developed a cultural resistance to hiring non-Goth people into that workplace, limiting their choices of available talent drastically.

Another example involves a major national potato grower who is a client of mine. The gentleman who was in charge of their farms was on what I would call a *lunar orbit* around the business. In other words, everybody else worked as growers and packers of potato products except him. The guy on the farm refused to participate and align with any strategic plan, because he thought his job was so important that he didn't feel that there was the need to participate. Nor would he submit to any functional reporting, meeting, or anything like that. He just went on doing things his own way, at his own pace and in his own time.

He survived in the company until the CEO and board found that he had been using company resources for his own interests. Had the CEO challenged this individual earlier and required alignment to their culture and plan, the outcome might have been different.

THE PENN STATE STORY

My final example involves Penn State University. Penn State University has gone through a lot of media controversy in the past three years with respect to Jerry Sandusky and his abuse of male children. He was convicted and sentenced to a term in jail.

Sandusky was an assistant coach under Joe Paterno. I would describe Penn State as a "good ol' boy" culture, especially in the sports department. Joe Paterno was so powerful that he was able to influence many aspects of the university. As a result, the culture in the football program was different from the culture elsewhere within the university. I'm not saying it was good or bad. I'm just saying it was different. It was like a separate country with a separate culture, just for the sports department.

This is where the problems began.

Penn State University is an institution of higher learning

first and foremost. It's not a football school, it's an institution of higher learning. What I believe happened was that a culture grew in an organization where people were afraid to speak out for fear they might lose their jobs.

I have no idea whether Paterno knew what was going on or not but there was a fear-based culture which meant no one would speak up. Maybe it was unintended on his part, but it caused people to fail to speak out about the abuse issue, even when they knew it was going on. As a result, everybody was held at arm's length because the football program was special and people within it were almost untouchable. Leaders felt it was important to maintain the brand instead of doing what was right.

It's not a good thing when organizations have an individual or a group of individuals who break away and make their own culture. They make their own rules, and that might be okay for a short time, but cannot really last.

I think that's what happened at Penn State and now they paid the price. They got sanctioned by the NCAA, had to pay a $60 million fine, and can't go to bowl games – which loses them a bunch of money. Recently, the NCAA lifted the sanctinos. The impact on the institution has been immense.

The biggest issue that they faced was that they almost

lost their accreditation as a university.

THE WRONG PEOPLE IN THE ROOM

Another issue is when you effectively have the wrong people in the room.

Certain people can look forward over a longer time span. These are people who can see further down the road naturally. They have an ability to think more strategically, to see a little further.

The people with a shorter-term focus tend to be doers. They're just there in the moment, living in the day. That's okay. We need everybody, and these points of view can be complementary.

The problem occurs where the doers and the visionary people sit down at the same table and try and communicate, and it's like using two different languages. Imagine somebody is speaking Swedish and somebody is speaking Cantonese. Their verbs and nouns are not the same, and even if they speak through translators, the exact meaning of an idiom can be lost.

Say a visionary says "soon" and a live-in-the-moment person says "soon." They think they are in agreement, but the word "soon" might mean "in a month or so" to the

OK, LET'S FOCUS
ON THE POSITIVES!

visionary while the live-in-the-day person believes it means "tomorrow." What this lack of compatibility does is to create an impasse and a lack of movement. Unfortunately, though both kinds of people are valuable, they just don't work out well in the same room.

For example, I work with a large specialty catering company. It does big weddings and a variety of events. In its strategic planning session we had a group of people which included some salespeople, some operational people, the leadership team and some administrative staff. In the room I'm guessing less than 50% of the people were really strategic in their ability to look forward and 50% were short-term thinkers. Of course, they came into conflict. As a facilitator you have to try to keep focused on strategy. This team kept going into the weeds. In the worst case scenario, you might have to eliminate some team members from the planning process – those people who are not strategic in a graceful way. Unfortunately, just because somebody is a key executive, it doesn't mean that they're a strategic thinker. In fact, this might be a left-brained person, who's doing all that operational stuff because they're good with timelines and charts.

One of the major issues is there's a tendency for non-strategic thinkers to just go tactical all the time. In other words, rather than thinking further ahead in the way the visionaries do, they want to know what they're going to do tomorrow, and how it's going to impact them. They don't understand that the point of the plan is to establish the goal or vision and then work out the steps to achieve that vision. They don't understand that they will indeed find out what they're going to do tomorrow because that is also a part of the plan.

FAILURE TO IMPLEMENT

One surprisingly common problem is the failure to implement. Often, while the leadership has good intentions, they get caught up in the day-to-day running of the company. They fail to refer back to the dashboard consistently – or to build the dashboard in the first place!

As a result, their staff doesn't take the plan seriously, either.

It gets really bad when the leadership goes through several attempts to implement a strategic plan without tangible results. I go see these kinds of clients six or eight months later and they say, "Well, nothing's happened, we haven't had time to do it, we've been too busy running the business."

You need to develop a plan of such size, scope and initiatives that an organization is ready, willing, and able to execute it.

THE CSSI STORY

One of the first plans I did was for a high-tech firm called CSSI. The CEO asked me to help, and we began the process of working on the plan. They had six or seven people in the room, and one of the issues that presented itself in my advance research was that the people within the organization felt they were in a quagmire. Nothing ever got done. They talked about a lot of stuff, had great ideas and vision, but they didn't execute. They were simply treading water.

At our first meeting, we talked about vision and values and the concept of enthusiasm and engagement throughout an organization. At the second meeting, I came back and there was an insurrection in the group because basically they said, "We don't know why we're even doing this. We never execute on anything we do anyway, so why should this be any different? Why should we even do this?" They then tuned out the conversation. We ended the planning process.

Next, the CEO of that company and I had to have some serious conversations. He was actually part of the problem because he approached every opportunity from a *tactical* standpoint (as a series of tactics) rather than setting up a *strategy*. As a result of the CEO's thinking style, that company had never employed a strategy. The company is usually successful – and full credit to the CEO, because he has a great vision – but they'd become stuck.

In the end he figured out that he was not the guy to take the company to the next level, so he's hired a president to come in and run the company. This new president, a strategic thinker, was engaged to put a strategic plan together. With the new guy in charge, maybe this time it will work out. Maybe they'll come up with some strategies they can execute.

THE RADIO FREE EUROPE STORY

I worked with a guy who had been CEO of Radio Free Europe. Radio Free Europe broadcasts into countries where government controls all media content. It is a high-purpose organization located in Prague. There are 650 people in an office there, and the issue centered around their leadership team. Without team alignment, you have difficulty executing a plan.

There's a lot of dysfunction created by a lack of focus and alignment. People are unsure of their roles, so they're searching for their best role, or trying to find where they fit in. Without direction, people ultimately fill the void with whatever they want. People are good at creating drama. They want to create their own space where they're in charge and if you're not telling them what to do they will do this, especially if they're strong people.

In this case, these were a variety of leaders from all over the world, so it was a mix of different cultural issues and different leadership issues. The major problem was created because leadership had a clear vision and purpose, but was unclear on the specifics of a plan, along with the roles and responsibilities of each leader.

TOO MANY COOKS

Another common problem is putting too many people in the room. A group of 12-15 people is about the right size. You need the key leaders, influencers and the strongest strategic thinkers. If they can't work together, they're out!

Let me give you an example.

THE ASSOCIATION

I worked with a statewide association to develop their strategic plan. They put 80 people in a room to develop this plan, trying to represent every aspect of their association. 80 people!

There were members that were from large stakeholders, associate companies, and smaller locally-owned members. These small members were present in much greater numbers than the representatives from the large ones. I soon discovered that although they were all in the same business, their interests were not particularly aligned and could not reasonably become so.

Long story short, the problems they faced were not the same, and the larger entities really had a difficult time. We had a difficult time finding any kind of consensus. The plan itself had elements that softened up the results, because we couldn't merge their desires together in a way that would be meaningful for the entire organization. It was a case of one plan *not* fitting all, and any compromise plan would be likely to fit none.

There were far too many people, all with differing angles on the process, and with different hopes for the results. The executive team was not in control. In this circumstance, you're going to have a difficult time getting to the next point, whatever that might happen to be, let alone coming to a satisfactory conclusion.

CHANGE OF LEADERSHIP

Another problem that comes up from time to time is that, having created a strong strategic plan and engaged the entire company, the leadership changes its mind. Of course, it's hard to turn team around once they're excited about their plan, their purpose and the implementation. Here's a quick example.

THE REDWOOD STORY

In this particular case, a friend of mine went into a planning process with a company in Silicon Valley in California. The company had thirty or so people in it. My friend helped set up this plan over two days spent among the redwood trees, as you can only do in California.

So here was he, along with the thirty or so people, coming up with a brilliant plan with driving purpose, plotting a way forward for this company. The business had been going along fine in the financial sense, but now they wanted to add purpose to that.

Everyone was excited and enthusiastic about the

plan and my friend saw what looked like a huge leap in engagement. It seemed like the job was done, but just a few weeks after that the guy who ran the company *sold it*. He must have been in negotiations even before the planning session was held, but never shared that with my friend or the other people in the company.

He sold the company to this big guy with a cigar, and this big guy with a cigar took my friend aside, because he was in an executive position there. In fact, he was probably one of the key executives there. He took him out along a jetty in Santa Cruz and he said, "My boy, the reason I bought this company is because you're in it."

And my friend said, "You know, that's fine, as long as we implement the strategic plan that we recently created together. That's what we're committed to."

And the guy with the cigar said, "About that plan..."

My friend had a bad feeling about this, so he waited to see what was coming next. Sure enough, the guy said, "I really only want to make money from this business so all that other *purpose* stuff that you're doing is irrelevant."

Now, my friend wasn't up for working with someone with that attitude, so he quit, and after that, *70% of the team went with him*. What an epic fail!

Section Five

Success Stories

In section four, we focused on what *can* go wrong. Most of the time, however, things go very well indeed! Here are some stories of success, along with my thoughts on why these particular companies enjoyed such strong results.

THE ORTHOPEDIC STORY

Success usually follows when **your executive leadership team is strongly focused on the process**. In other words, you need to get your senior leadership to be very dedicated and focused on driving the process. When senior leadership is focused on aligning the organization on a plan going forward with some vision, that's when things go best.

One example is an orthopedic implant company which is a distributor for a major national manufacturer. They sell hip, knee, shoulder and joint replacement products made by Zimmer Holdings, along with some other products. This local distributor had grown dramatically over a number of years to more than 40 million dollars in annual revenue – without ever having a budget or any strategic plan at all!

We did the *Fast Track Strategic Planning* process together, developed a plan for them, and really got their senior leadership team aligned. It turned out that the plan, along with their ability to execute, was like rocket fuel for this company. That organization continued its double-digit growth for the next five or seven years, during which they cruised to north of a $100 million in annual revenue!

The owner of that distributorship eventually was able to retire happily.

THE KLINE'S STORY

Another success story comes from an organization that I dealt with maybe seven years ago. It is a waste water management company called Kline's Services.

One of the elements to the Kline's business is to clean grease traps in restaurants. It's not very glamorous work. It turns out that every restaurant you go to has a grease trap where they pour all the grease from the day's cooking. I know, it doesn't sound too appealing but I guess it prevents the grease from clogging up the sinks, pipes and drains.

What Kline's does is to go in and pressure wash the traps and clean them out. They take that grease and convert it in to something that's sustainable in the world.

When Kline's began the planning process, they had around 300 restaurants as clients, but no clear strategy to increase that number. They had no contracts with the restaurants, and they had no specific plan. They just went to these places when their grease traps needed cleaning.

As part of our strategic plan, they looked to expand their footprint to include a larger slice of South Central Pennsylvania. In addition, they decided to establish bundled pricing, so they would offer people higher levels of service if they had a regular contract. This was a good way of consolidating existing business and maybe gaining some new business too.

With the senior team fully engaged in the plan, they went from 300 restaurants to over 1000 in a very short period of time. The strategic plan made an incredible difference, because this grease trap cleaning bundle was one of the highest margin items that they were able to sell. It made a difference in some of the other commodity-driven work that they did. You look at a huge success story like this and you say, "That's a pretty big thing and they did it."

As you can see, the *Fast Track Strategic Planning* process can be very effective indeed.

WRAPPING UP

And so we come to the end of this book.

As you know, my intention in writing this book has been to create a primer that will help you take something that seems very complex and long and difficult, and make it feel reasonable and bite-sized. Strategic planning sounds like an awfully big job when you consider you're looking three to five years ahead. This is especially true when you consider how circumstances might change in those years.

With this in mind, I broke the process down into 8 easy steps, detailed in Section Two. If you follow the steps by doing the exercises one by one, you'll have your own *Fast Track Strategic Plan* in the end.

Now I hope you'll have a good grasp on the following points.

- What Strategic Planning is, and why it's important.

- Why it's important to do it swiftly.

- A plan is a living document and that it is likely to be in a constant state of evolution.

- There are eight steps that are designed to be bite-sized steps that really anyone can wrap their mind around.

- These eight steps lead towards a goal or vision of the way the organization could be at the end of three to five years.

- The goal or vision should be a people-based story.

- The goal should be encapsulated in a statement of purpose or slogan that is around fifteen words in length.

- This purpose should be known, discussed and circulated through all levels of the organization. It should become *our story*; something to own and to be proud of.

- By the end of this book, you should be in an optimum place to have your own pages, and be well on the way to your own *Fast Track Strategic Plan*.

You'll also be armed with examples of what works and what doesn't and, importantly, why things work or don't.

Finally, I hope all of this is as useful as possible for as many people as possible. I hope many businesses both small and large will go through this process and enjoy the benefits of having their own *Fast Track Strategic Plan*.

And of course, please get in touch through my website www.johndame.com and let me know how it's going!

Yours,

John Dame

NEVER MIND MY PALM –
LET ME TELL YOU ABOUT
THE FUTURE OF *YOUR* BUSINESS!

Made in the USA
Middletown, DE
18 August 2019